From the
TRENCHES

stories + anecdotes + insights
from in-house creative leaders

LEADERSHIP VOLUME TWO

From the Trenches

stories + anecdotes + insights: From in-house creative leaders

Acknowledgements

Thank you to all who made Leadership Volume Two
a fun and seamless process, again!

Editorial Director	Kim Kiser
Copy Editor	Vivian Fransen
2-Minute Tips	Kim Kiser
Illustrator	Mark Cole
Case Study	Robin Colangelo
Discussions	David Howland
	Alberta Testanero
Cover Design	Eileen Riestra
Cover Image	ShutterStock
Layout Design	Robin Colangelo
	Ava Salazar
Articles	Andy Brenits
	Carol Carter
	Jereme Clymer
	Nathalie Heywood Smith
	Kevin Alan Mau
	Eileen Riestra
	Martin Schott
	Jim Woods
Preferred Partners	Brilliant Graphics
	Dog and Pony Studios

FOREWORD:
Ken Carbone: From the Outside Looking In

The word objectivity is apparently full of subjectivity. In looking
for a quote to use in this foreword, I found a colorful mix of examples.
Noted psychologist Abraham Maslow offers: "Dispassionate objectivity is
itself a passion, for the real and for the truth." Celebrated photographer
Annie Leibovitz who is known to get close to her subjects claims: "I no
longer believe there is such a thing as objectivity." British novelist
Jonathan Coe says: "Objectivity is just male subjectivity."

For decades our agency has brought our brand of objectivity to
companies large and small. But we also fully appreciate the value of
the inside perspective to help address a given challenge. Whether it is
a brand identity, website or recruiting campaign, our outside view has
always focused on discovering valuable opportunities that might be
overlooked simply because the in-house team is "too close to the
problem." However, the combination of seamless collaboration, clarity
in role responsibility and a unified vision for success is the winning
formula that has defined some of our best work.

I have been very fortunate to have worked with some stellar in-house
teams and CMOs to produce strategic design solutions for a range
of complex challenges. These three examples are a blend of fact and
fiction. They reflect relationships and lasting impressions from years
of experience:

VERY GOOD: Meet "Melody Monroe," VP of Communications
Melody is very organized, energetic, a consensus builder and a solid
planner. Although relatively new to her position, she is tasked with
launching a major recruiting campaign. She uses the added muscle of
an outside design firm to help win over the company leadership, who
is marketing-averse and very budget-conscious. With this in mind, she
chooses a cost-effective design approach that will attract top talent
and not be creatively "threatening" to management. She is looking for

a solid win with the hope of building trust and autonomy for her design and marketing role within the company. The campaign results are very positive, and management congratulates her on her effort.

EVEN BETTER: Meet "John Jackson," EVP Creative Services
After an exciting merger, the CEO of John's company enlists his help in planning a brand identity "refresh." John, who has successfully launched a rebrand for his previous employer, prepares an RFP for the assignment and sends it to three design agencies. After credential presentations, John advises management in the selection process and recommends a firm. The design consultant receives one of the best creative briefs ever and works closely with John's team to carefully plan a year-long rebranding process. Roles and responsibilities are defined, key milestones are established, budget parameters are clarified and strategies for winning management approval are determined. John is ready to go and sets the project in motion.

JUST GREAT: Meet "Susan Sharpe," Chief Marketing Officer
Three words best describe Susan: courageous, collaborative and committed. She demands cutting-edge work and is not afraid to bleed. She understands that the greatest rewards come from carefully managing risk and has gained a very high level of trust from her CEO. She has the right to be demanding because she will put her neck on the line for "great" work and bristles at the word "good." She values design and sees her agency as a true partner, not a "vendor." Together, they present a compelling case for design as a competitive advantage that convinces her CFO that great creative is an essential investment in the company brand. She is a fighter. She is a star.

The knowledge an in-house design and marketing department has is absolutely essential to set the context for any assignment.
The objective view and diverse experience provided by a design agency will reveal unexpected solutions to problems. Building a bond of trust,

aligning goals and generating creative enthusiasm between the two entities are what it takes to insure measurable success. Of this, I'm absolutely certain but that might just be male subjectivity!

Ken Carbone
Co-Founder
Carbone Smolan Agency

Ken Carbone is a designer, artist, musician, author and teacher. As the co-founder and Chief Creative Director of the Carbone Smolan Agency, he is among America's most respected graphic designers, whose work is renowned for its substance and style. Under his design ethos to "unify, simplify, amplify," Ken has built an international reputation creating outstanding design programs for a world-class clientele that includes W Hotels, Morgan Stanley, Christie's, Tiffany & Co., Mandarin Oriental Hotel Group and Canon, as well as celebrated institutions such as the Museum of Modern Art, The High Museum, Natural History Museum of Los Angeles and the Musée du Louvre.

Ken is the co-author of Dialog: What Makes a Great Design Partnership, which celebrates the 35-year collaboration with his partner Leslie Smolan. He is a professor in the Masters in Branding and MFA programs at the School of Visual Arts in New York City, and is a featured blogger for Fast Company magazine and The Huffington Post.

In 2014, Ken received the AIGA Medal for an outstanding career of excellence in design.

Table of Contents

TABLE OF CONTENTS

Welcome...

to "Leadership Volume Two" for in-house creative leaders.

Inside you'll find fresh ideas to spark your inspiration in creative leadership, brand management and strategic design that can help you solve today's business challenges.

We see this book as the second edition of many more to come. This and future books will present the latest in-house tips and trends from a variety of industry voices. Content is written and curated by experienced in-house leaders—leaders who have built creative teams all over, uniting the worlds of business and design.

This compilation of thought leadership articles, tips and interviews was created by a group of in-house design leaders who believe in supporting and evolving the efforts of in-house design professionals.

For more than 10 years, InSource has been committed to creative leadership excellence and effective business management, providing a platform to share ideas and practices among leaders of in-house creative teams. Our goal is to enhance the value that in-house creative teams add to their organizations and brands.

We hope you'll enjoy this collection of practical insights as one of the many ways we reach out to one another as peers in our ongoing pursuit of design management excellence.

Andy Brenits
President, InSource

Robin Colangelo
Vice President, InSource

Is Your Predecessor Preventing Your Success?

Ah, the excitement of starting a new job! After months of applications and many rounds of interviews, the offer to build, lead and grow a new team finally comes through. You are excited to be moving upward in your career, or maybe just on to a new challenge where all of your best talents and experiences can be put to use.

During your first few days on the job you spend plenty of time learning—learning about the business, meeting lots of new people and diving into how things get done in your new department. And that's when you start to learn about how things were before...

The "what was" problem

At some point within your first two weeks, you start to hear the stories of the past. Some of these stories will be positive, even funny, about how great things are due to a team that meshes really well. You will hear about happy clients, award-winning work and the hard road it took to get there. Some of these stories, however, will be less positive— stories about a team that was not motivated, not collaborative and not responsive to the needs of the internal clients. You might even hear about how high of a turnover there has been in the department. All of these things, both good and bad, happened because of your predecessor.

You've got big shoes to fill

Let's say your predecessor was the kind of leader who just killed it. He did a great job keeping the team engaged, the work interesting and the clients happy. As the new replacement leader coming on board, you have big shoes to fill. Chances are your predecessor was not only good at his job, but he was well liked to boot (pun intended).

In this case, you're coming into a group that—while perhaps excited to see you—might be a bit leery of what you're going to bring to the table. After all, how can things really get any better for this team when it's already pretty great? In other words, once the new-guy shine wears off in week four, everyone will be looking at you like "So what can you offer us that the old guy we loved so much didn't already do?"

You've walked into a minefield

On the other hand, let's say things were not so great when your predecessor left. Maybe that's the reason he is no longer there in the first place. The team could be any one, or more, of the following: unhappy, unmotivated, uninspired, unruly, uncreative, insubordinate, disorganized and/or overworked. And the clients? They don't like working with your department because of all the reasons I just listed.

So how are you going to fix this? You, my friend, have a long road ahead of you. But, like Mount Everest, you can get to the summit; it's just going to be a long road to get there, and it will take a lot of hard work.

What's a new leader to do?

Of course, you could also be lucky enough to have been asked to start a new in-house creative team. In this case, you don't have any of the history of a predecessor to worry about, but you still need to take into consideration how the business operated before you came on board.

No matter what the scenario is for you, below are five suggestions when starting your new leadership gig:

NUMBER 1: Don't change anything

Things may or may not be working as well as you hoped when you walk in the door on your first day. For better or for worse, your team is still operating. Throwing a wrench into the works early on could do more harm than good.

NUMBER 2: Be observant, and listen as much as you talk

You're a leader, so you might be tempted to take charge of the situation to make your mark. Don't. Instead, learn as much as you can about the business and current state of affairs before you discuss potential changes with your boss.

NUMBER 3: Be patient, and have a plan
Unless there are extreme circumstances requiring an immediate change, develop a plan for improving your operations and get buy-in on it from above and below.

NUMBER 4: Stop interviewing for the job
Resist the urge to remind everyone how much you know or what you've done before to handle a similar situation. The person who hired you knows that, and has probably told your team and peers already. You don't have as much to prove as you think you do. Simply do what you were hired to do.

NUMBER 5: Build relationships
A big part of leading a team, and its clients, is knowing who you're working with. Take time to get to know people and learn what drives them. It will not only help you be successful, but it will help you gain agreement on your improvement plans later on.

Let hindsight truly be 20/20
After taking the leadership reins a number of times in my career due to promotions or starting with a new company, I can say that I have some perspective on this, so my last piece of advice is this: Don't get bogged down by "what was." You have to respect the history of how things were B.Y. (before you), but you can't let history bog you down. Learn from it, but don't let anyone dwell on the past. Build your own history, and make your own mark.

(This article was previously published on in-source.org.)

Andy Brenits
President, InSource
Principal, Brenits Creative

Andy Brenits is a left-brained creative who is as comfortable analyzing metrics and developing processes as he is developing creative strategy. An inspired creative business leader, Andy is accomplished at building and leading teams that deliver exceptional business results and creative ideas.

He's passionate about the creative process and how it can be used to drive strategic business goals, and has been delivering thought leadership, creative solutions and design thinking for 20 years. Andy has been working on the InSource Board of Directors since 2007 and has served as its President since 2010.

Getting to "Why"
A common challenge for in-house creative teams is transitioning from order takers to strategic partners. If this doesn't describe your team, think about who is pulling the weight—just your handful of senior members? How can you get everyone on the team contributing strategically?

One place to start is training everyone to uncover the "why" behind each request. The folks sending work your department's way are notorious for calling you up with the "what"—I need a brochure, a slide deck, a video, a web page. As a service group, it's tempting to hop right on the request and get them what they are asking for—to "take the order."

Instead, ask them why they need it. Once you uncover the objective of the piece, how it will be used and who the audience is, you'll often find that what they are asking for isn't what they need. Coming up with creative alternatives that solve the problem proves to be not only more valuable to the business, but also more satisfying for your team.

Kim Kiser

What Makes a Creative Project the Best Ever?

SHARED IDEAS

When I was barely 18 years old, my world was all about football, the latest Commodores release and cruising the El Camino Réal in my old pickup truck. I was also known as the go-to guy for party flyers and underground cartoons. Even though I was creatively inclined since I could pick up a crayon, I had no idea what graphic design was, or that someone actually made a living doing it.

At the same time, my older brother was in the United States Air Force. He was stationed at Edwards Air Force Base in the California desert. I thought that was very cool because of the base's reputation of being where all of the latest fighter jets were tested. I pictured the skies full of the best pilots in the world performing all kinds of craziness above the dry lake bed.

When the summer break came, my brother asked if I wanted to come spend a week on base with him. I jumped at the chance.

I found Edwards to be an amazing place. My brother drove me around to see all the coolest stuff—some of which I wasn't really sure I should be seeing. I was awestruck, but not nearly as much as I would be in time.

One afternoon, my brother drove me out to the edge of the dry lake. It seemed like we were driving forever, then way off in the distance a tiny orange structure appeared. The structure seemed to grow exponentially as we got closer. When we finally got to it, I saw it was enormous.

The structure was the lifting mechanism that raised the space shuttle for mounting on the back of a Boeing 747. But what was thrilling was the vehicle parked at its base. It was the Columbia, back from its fourth mission. I was staring at more history than I could have ever dreamed.

Years later, my family and I were living in Southern California. I was just outside my front door when I looked up and noticed the largest contrail I had ever seen. It looked different. It was brownish, and there were odd specs amid the trail. I could hear the television from inside the house, and I realized I was witnessing the complete destruction of the space shuttle. It was the Columbia. History again unfolded before my own eyes. I was working for Boeing at the time.

I was still with Boeing eight years later when the space shuttle flew for the last time. This time, it was the Atlantis. If I had been told 30 years beforehand that in that moment on that beautiful day in the desert I would be designing the Boeing commemorative merchandise for the 30th anniversary of the space shuttle, and its final voyage, I wouldn't have been able to comprehend it—from a professional, historic or emotional perspective.

As a creative, was that the best project I ever had the privilege to work on? There's no question.

Kevin Alan Mau

Brand and Creative Strategist
The Boeing Company

As a Senior Creative Director at The Boeing Company, Kevin Alan Mau has found inspiration and energy from leading creative teams and being involved in the stewardship and evolution of a global brand. Working with the aerospace giant since 1997, he has also designed, directed or strategized on the development of marketing and communication materials for most of the global icons we all know, including the Space Shuttle, International Space Station and commercial airplanes such as the 747 Jumbo Jet, the new 787 Dreamliner and the 737, the world's most popular airplane.

Before Boeing, Kevin developed creative solutions for various companies—large and small—as an independent design consultant. His key clients included the Chamber of Commerce in Campbell, California; the Watsonville Air Show; West Coast Antique Aircraft Museum; Varian Associates; Litton Solid State; and various local mom-and-pop shops.

Kevin is a vocal advocate for the arts and design, both for Boeing and the outside world.

Five Things I Wish a Mentor Had Told Me

We can all benefit from mentors—especially those who share our passion for the profession. But mentors don't always find you when you need them. Like any other significant people in our lives, they tend to enter and leave our lives more by chance and circumstance.

While I had mentors later in my career, I didn't have one at the start. So if I were mentoring my younger self, these are the things I would have focused on:

NUMBER 1: Be creative about collaboration
Collaborative work environments are a hallmark of many successful companies today. Diverse, inclusive companies draw on the best ideas from employees, have the best output and bring benefits to the bottom line.

Collaboration among team members is something that in-house and external agencies often do, but collaborating directly with your clients during the creative process is less common. I would argue, however, that this is an added benefit, in your client's eye, of having you in-house.

When staff and time are tight, walking over to an internal client sitting down the hall or sharing your screen with a colleague in another office to review some early work can not only save time but get your client feeling part of the process—a true partner and collaborator.

When you work as part of an in-house agency, this partnership with real-time review and collaboration is your special sauce. If you don't take advantage of the interpersonal connectivity, you are missing out on an opportunity to demonstrate the value you bring; you lose an opportunity to deepen your knowledge base and you lose the chance to better understand your client.

Takeaway: Don't be afraid to collaborate in real time with your clients. You will end up with better results and more collegial relationships.

NUMBER 2: Build your team for future growth

When you are part of a small group, you need to be resourceful out of necessity and you find yourself wearing multiple hats—graphic designer, account manager, traffic coordinator, operations director, administrator—and the list goes on.

As you grow, you need to start bringing in people who will help you not only accommodate the demands of today but better prepare you for the needs of tomorrow.

While it may be tempting to hire people who are expert in the need you have today, consider hiring people who are skilled and talented in growth areas that provide new opportunities to learn. As your team grows and evolves, you will need people to learn new skills and take on new tasks until you can bring in more headcount.

When you hire people who are capable of doing more than what is currently being asked, you will be able to take on the challenges of tomorrow first with the team you already have in place and then later with those you will bring in. In the meanwhile, you will be growing the skill-set of your existing team and preparing them for leadership opportunities as you bring in additional staff.

Takeaway: Hire today for the team you want in place tomorrow.

NUMBER 3: Understand the value that you bring

As employees of your firm, you know more about your products, your services and your brand than any outside agency. You participate in management town halls, you live and breathe your brand principles, you talk to your colleagues about business plans and goals and you read company news on your Intranet pages.

You probably also have a tremendous history with your brand. Chances are you've been involved in re-brands, campaigns and acquisitions that have helped your brand evolve over time.

What's more, you have relationships with your clients that run deeper than a meeting once a week. You pass each other in the halls, you see each other for lunch or the occasional happy hour and you chat when you are getting your morning cup of coffee.

So if you are a member of an in-house team and you aren't using those relationships to get better insight and foster richer collaboration that will ultimately result in better creative output, you are missing out on a key differentiator for yourself and your team.

You have "insider information," and if you use that correctly, you should have the advantage over any outside firm. Make sure you bring that information to the table for every project you work on. Ask yourself: What value can I bring to this creative challenge that stems directly from my experience as an employee?

Takeaway: Understand the value that you bring to your organization and capitalize on it.

NUMBER 4: Keep your operations efficient and transparent

I'm a relatively recent convert to the power and beauty of operational excellence. I say that because it was just two years ago when we established a dedicated operations function within the team. To be honest, prior to that time, I thought that using a senior role to fill a non-creative post was extravagant. It is hard keeping up with the internal demand for our services—so I thought the best way to use any additional headcount would be in a creative role. But I was wrong. When we got close to a 50-person team, we were told by an outside consultant that we needed an operations manager to help us perform better and define metrics on our performance. We took their report to our CMO and got the OK to hire an ops manager.

Our focus on operations has resulted in increased transparency through regular metrics and reporting that has given us credibility with our management team when asking for resources, both human and hardware.

The transparency has helped take the mystery out of what we do and why we do it. The more people within our organization who know about how we spend our time, the better it is for our team. If we are working hard and working smart, giving people a chance to look under the hood into what we are doing and how we do it, at the least, makes them more understanding of the demands on our time and, at the most, provides justification for additional resources.

Takeaway: Creative may be the star of the show, but good operations keep the lights on.

NUMBER 5: Learn to be comfortable—and thrive with ambiguity
Good firms experience change some of the time but great firms seem to experience almost constant change.

Constant change means that roles and responsibilities are in flux. It means the way we did something yesterday may not work today. It means we need to constantly adapt and respond to changing demands and challenges. It means we should never feel comfortable that we have it all figured out.

It is easier to do our jobs when they are neatly outlined. But it is not so easy when things are changing and we still need to move ahead quickly. For some people, this just doesn't sit right. The ambiguity angers them, frustrates them and renders them incapable of moving ahead.

But if you are in a firm that is growing and changing, **you need to learn to be comfortable with ambiguity. Not only be comfortable with it, but learn to thrive with it.** And I would go even further to say you should be thankful for it. If you are in a company that experiences ambiguity, chances are your company is changing to better respond to the current environment and will continue to grow. Ultimately, this should mean more opportunity for you and your colleagues in the months and years ahead.

Takeaway: Learn to be comfortable with ambiguity. If you can excel in situations where there is transition and reinvention taking place, you will have a role to play in any firm.

Carol Carter
BlackRock
Global Head of Creative Services

Reporting to the Global Head of Brand, Carol Carter is Global Head of Creative Services for BlackRock, where she directs an in-house design team responsible for developing creative solutions that support the firm's marketing strategies.

Prior to taking on her current responsibilities, Carol was Head of Account Management and Production for the Creative Services team. She previously held marketing and publicity roles for Merrill Lynch. Before joining the financial services industry, she worked as a reporter and editor for various newspapers and magazines in the New York City area.

Rebranding InSource

The why, what and how

Due to the fast and furious growth within the in-house community, President Andy Brenits and Vice President Robin Colangelo of InSource got together to brainstorm how to better support the in-house creative community. What do they really need?

Our answers were simple. The in-house community needs more tools and thought leadership to provoke and inspire creative leaders to build and lead their teams fearlessly. Building today's in-house agency is no easy task, but with the proper support, guidance and tools in your pocket, you can accomplish anything.

Refreshing InSource's brand to keep up with the latest trends in the market, such as responsive web design with modern photography and slick graphics, will allow InSource initiatives to shine.

When several thousand brand advocates are your audience, it's generally a best practice to have a savvy brand. So Andy and I took a hard look at what we were doing, what we looked like and how we sounded. We set out to begin our rebrand journey in late 2014 and are finally feeling like we are at the finish line.

Our Board members are brand advocates, creative leaders and innovative business professionals who work on the best brands in the world and possess a wealth of knowledge. So we spoke with our Board of Directors and picked their brains for ideas first, then we reached out into our networks for advice and some initial thoughts.

We knew our visual identity was way past its prime, but you know how the saying goes: "The cobbler's children have no shoes." Yes, a terrible excuse to let your brand go downhill, but just being honest really.

We were also painfully aware that we had outgrown the look and technology of our website. Andy's main concern was that our technology was no longer keeping up with our membership demands. My main concern was the need to look savvy to attract our current audience and new members.

Website

First, we tackled our website, which was our biggest and, of course, most complicated asset. Shani Sandy evoked the services of Dog and Pony Studios to overhaul our old WordPress site into a fresh and responsive design. The Board voted on our new theme after reviewing several options, and the team at Dog and Pony Studios began the race to the finish line. Our old site was migrated into our new template with the notion that imagery, graphics and content would improve over time. (More on this later.)

Visual identity

Then we tackled our visual identity and messaging. Yes, some may say we worked backwards, but sometimes you do what you can, when you can. As a nonprofit, we decided to move forward even if out of order. As branding professionals, we know how to catch up and make this work.

Ava Salazar and Eileen Riestra stepped up to the plate to take on our stodgy visual identity challenge. The two design gurus met, reviewed, brainstormed and concepted until out came the winning idea.

Ava and Eileen presented their findings on who InSource was, who our audience was and where we could take our brand. Andy and I were so excited that these two generous and talented individuals took the initiative to work together on this major challenge and came up with exactly where we think we should be.

We retained our identity by sticking with our logo and color palette and putting all efforts into changing up our photography and graphics. Our graphics are now easier to read, slicker looking and contemporary.

Our photography now resembles real people to depict our real members. Since our organization is all about YOU, we wanted to look and feel like something any one of us could quickly relate to. Thanks to Shutterstock, we now have a pool of fresh images that look like approachable people doing their thing inside of the graphic design industry. Converting our images to grayscale allows the imagery to feel more sophisticated and makes our PMS 186 really pop.

Messaging

Then we took a look at our messaging. Are we hitting it out of the park on our social media splash pages, in our articles and in our headlines? Not so much.

Kim Kiser and Shani Sandy from our Board gave us some advice on language and wording to improve SEO. Why not tackle both issues together! Our messaging had become too wordy in some areas and too complicated to skim through easily. Basically, we needed to get to the point faster and friendlier in a modern voice.

The grand finale

As one last step, we went back for a round two website enhancement to put the icing on the cake. Now that we had our VI in line and knew better what we really needed from a technology standpoint to enhance the organization for members, we were able to finalize the site. The new look and feel follows our refreshed branding, has improved CMS, a rebuilt member directory, online forms and forum portals, plus improved responsiveness.

The entire process wasn't always so clear. We had long breaks in between small successes, and we had uncertain thoughts on what to do next, but at the end of the day, perseverance has turned this caterpillar into a butterfly right before our eyes.

We launched each initiative as it was complete, instead of waiting for one big reveal, to show our members and community that we are dedicated to forward movement.

From designers to developers to writers, we had support from all angles to get this brand refresh on the right track and lead it to launch. The project was a perfect example of a community coming together to make strides for the good of in-house design and leadership.

Robin Colangelo
VP Board of Directors, InSource
Global Director Creative Services, White & Case

Robin Colangelo is a strategic, results-oriented creative leader in developing and executing integrated brand strategies across print and digital communication channels. In her current role as Global Director of Creative Services, Robin leads the in-house creative team for White & Case, where she manages the visual identity and oversees a diverse team across six offices and five countries.

Since 2010 Robin has worked on the Board of InSource, serving as its Vice President since 2013. Her volunteer work on the Board encompasses driving strategy and process for the organization's initiatives and goals, in addition to heading up sponsorships.

DISCUSSION:
David Howland + Robin Colangelo

David Howland

Creative & Digital Strategy Leader
Nasdaq

David and I sat down for lunch in the Flatiron district in New York City at a trendy Mediterranean restaurant and quickly learned we have very similar leadership roles, even though our industries are miles apart.

We swapped stories about a day in the life, our biggest challenges and even some frightening management stories, which we'll spare you here.

Lucky for me, after lunch David warned me not to drink the full cup of Turkish coffee I ordered, which I never had before, or I would soon be wearing a coffee grind grill. Thanks for the heads-up, David!

Here's a few insights I learned from lunching with David:

Tell me about your career path. How did you get here?
I started as a cabinet maker in Seattle and now run creative and digital strategy for a Fortune 500 company in New York City. It's been quite a journey, and one with creative expression as a common theme throughout.

In-house roles have been on the rise for years. How has this affected you and your team?
The breadth of our impact is tremendous. We touch all aspects of the company and as such are one of the most well-informed internal groups. This results in a strong sense of mission and commitment with partnerships across all of our many business lines. It's critical to socialize and present the team as such, as one can't assume others will recognize how much the team is immersed in the business.

Are you noticing any new in-house trends?
Today, teams are asked to be equally adept across any number of different communications vehicles. What was once a printed annual report project has evolved to a digital-first approach with the printed, social, video, email and environmental components of a larger campaign

initiative all driven by the same team. What was once centered on creativity now emphasizes measurable engagement.

Is your team tasked with being your organization's Brand Advocates?

We are first and foremost the stewards of the brand, responsible for its health and vitality while always seeking to aggressively test and explore the boundaries. Our goal is to create a dynamic such that every employee is an evangelist of our brand and feels a strong sense of individual and collective ownership.

Does your company have a Chief Design role? If not, do you see this evolving in the future?

Nasdaq has a strong entrepreneurial and disruptive tenor where talent and drive are encouraged. I've been fortunate to be able to craft my current role, creating an opportunity and a position that previously did not exist. As such, anything's possible.

Where do you find leadership inspiration?

All around me, but specifically through direct interactions with colleagues and family. I spend more time now than ever before engaging with others to network and learn, yet it isn't nearly enough and is an area of focus moving forward. I've also become far more receptive to learn about new tools and services.

How do you set the tone for your team?

It's important that the team is confident and secure in my support. I want them to take risks, to challenge client assumptions and to take ownership over even the most basic project as portfolio-worthy material. Clear lines of communication, which include debriefs on larger corporate strategy and an understanding of the importance of their contributions, lead to a greater sense of mission and ability to collaborate effectively with clients.

What's your biggest in-house challenge?

Developing and maintaining a sound process. We are, as is common in our field, in a continuous cycle of aggressive project deadlines and demands. While a sound process won't solve everything, I believe it's crucial in reducing inefficiencies and surprises while positioning our creatives for success.

What has surprised you most about being in-house?

The range and amount of creative opportunity are tremendous. We touch all business lines and initiatives throughout the company, taking what is essentially a core brand and bringing it to life in new and inventive ways with each execution within a larger coordinated framework. With the additional challenge of purpose, we're more than just a creative team: We solve problems and define meaningful engagements.

Describe your team's most innovative project and how they got there.

In 2014, we rebranded. In just over a year's time, we launched a comprehensive new brand identity, positioning, advertising campaign and technology platform for our digital properties. It was an ambitious effort and involved the talents of many different people, including external agencies, while being driven by the different teams within our Marketing & Communications group.

Is your team functioning like an in-house agency?

We certainly strive to and are in the process now of evaluating where we need to improve and adopt new approaches.

Looking back 10 years, did you imagine you would be where you are?

Yes. I was already a Creative Director with extensive experience building and running websites. The confluence of digital and design was already well underway so I then viewed my current role as an aspirational opportunity.

So what's next for you?
Anyone need some cabinets or custom furniture?

A little more about David
David Howland has over 20 years of experience building and refining successful brands, driving online engagement and managing teams with a focus upon dynamic and lasting customer experiences. He currently runs the brand, creative and enterprise digital strategy for Nasdaq and is based in New York City. His previous roles include Creative Director for Case Western Reserve University and Assistant Curator and Art Director for the International Center of Photography. His passions include running, home brewing and, of course, woodworking.

2-MINUTE TIP

Twenty Questions

As a creative manager, it's likely you have a steady stream of people in your office (or hovering around your cubicle) all day long, barraging you with questions about what direction to take on a project, what to tell the client, how to prioritize workloads, etc. While your vision and decisiveness keeps the department moving, it can also breed laziness.

Next time someone on your team comes to you with a question, ask them what they think first. In fact, insist that no one come to you with a question—no matter how small—without presenting a few possible solutions of their own. Getting your team into the habit of problem solving empowers them and takes some of the load off of you.

That's a win-win.

Kim Kiser

Patience + Perseverance = Success

A few years ago I began working as the in-house marketing brand manager at a well-known wine company in New England. When I was hired, they did not have a structured marketing department or processes. The person in charge was an office assistant who thought she was a designer because she knew how to operate Adobe software programs. It is extremely difficult to work on a branding strategy when your co-workers have never seen an integrated approach to branding and design.

In this situation, my first impulse was to run! My instincts told me to find an environment where you can be appreciated and your work can be valued. This is a key turning point people often face at one time or another. The solution is to adopt the following approach:

1. Breathe in, breathe out.

2. Look beyond the immediate situation to the growth opportunity.

3. Recognize the potential for personal growth in Patience and Perseverance—two virtues that are necessary for true growth. I write them both with a capital "P" because these two virtues have accompanied me in every professional success I have had. I consider them absolutely essential, and the only way to acquire them is by habit, and under difficult circumstances.

The first major challenge my new boss had was finding the time to sit with me to tell me what the company really needed—not just the packaging or the promotional material they needed in a rush, but their overall need to communicate who they were through design. Taking the time for this level of strategic planning can be challenging, but it is essential for good design.

I decided I needed to reconstruct the marketing department, and what a challenge it was. First of all, my boss—the CEO of the company—was an accountant and knew all about Peachtree and Excel. It's amazing that I didn't get stuck designing for the company in Excel. I patiently took my time to prove—not by words, but by actions—what design was, how design would impact the business and how it could improve their return on investment (ROI) results. Because the CEO focused on ROI, we were now talking the same language so she was soon able to understand the value of design.

So how did I begin?
I went back to the basics. First, I eliminated any Word or Excel sell sheets that were on the server and started designing beautiful, visually impactful sell sheets. After I got the first "Ah, wow, what is this?" I knew I would eventually achieve success. After I redesigned the print materials, I started to digitalize them to create the same impact through email blasts, social media and, most importantly, the website.

Working on more than 1,500 products that needed branding soon became too much for only one designer. While I was breaking down barriers with the CEO, at the same time, I had developed a reputation as a Bulldog. Saying "no" to all of the company's bad habits had put me in a precarious position, but I knew I needed to ask for an additional designer.

The CEO was an individual who could generally calculate any cost in an instant. I thought it would take me months, maybe even years, to get a new hire approved. But I mustered up the courage and explained that in order to focus on brand development and keep up the growth pace we had begun, we needed someone who could maintain the daily tasks with consistency—someone who could make sure we didn't lose the ground we had already gained.

Miraculously, I got the approval I needed. We started the hiring process, and after two months we finally found the right candidate.

Pushing the team to get out of their comfort zone
As a leader, I try to constantly challenge my team to break through what I call the "glass ceiling of design." Many people can produce pretty graphics, but few can produce graphics that really communicate core concepts. So I gave the recently hired designer the most important project of the year for the company—a wine book for the Wine Show. The project involved producing information pages on the wines from all international and national wineries around the world that would be presented at the show. This was a big risk for the company and also for me. It was difficult for me to let the project go, because I had a high standard for it, had done it myself in the past and really didn't believe anyone could improve on it.

At the end of the day the project was successful, and the designer came up with new ideas I hadn't thought of. **The key was learning to let go.** I have learned that when you give people responsibility, when they sense they are valued, they will do their best work and will be challenged by the creative process.

Where are we now?
After almost a year leading the team, I am happy to report that the sales reps are now working more efficiently and the CEO has come to understand the importance of design thinking in the workforce. We also successfully developed the website, social media and print materials, which are having a significant impact on sales and the company's position in the industry.

Some people don't want to push themselves to the edge of design, and that's okay. In some ways, that's my job. But I still encourage designers to push beyond only production. I'm thinking of our work as art.

I'm thinking of the future. I want to invest in my people, if they are willing to take their work to the next level.

Eileen Riestra
Creative Director
DYASTUDIO, INC.

After working with a variety of international and local advertising agencies in Puerto Rico, Eileen Riestra, Creative Director, established DYASTUDIO, INC. with the intention of creating a firm that would primarily center on design and visual communications. In 2014, Eileen established Depict Brands, the sister company of DYASTUDIO, in Boston, Massachusetts, focusing on branding development and design related services that cater to the American and Hispanic markets.

Eileen holds a bachelor's degree of Fine Arts in graphic design from The New England School of Art and Design at Suffolk University in Boston, Massachusetts. In 2012, she earned a certificate in Executive Education from the Yale School of Management, and in July 2013, she attended the master designer intensive workshop with world-renowned design leader Massimo Vignelli. In October 2013, Eileen won a Hispanic Graphic Design Award from GDUSA.

▌2-MINUTE TIP

Staff Development

Staff development is one of those responsibilities all managers will agree is important. Almost all managers will also agree it's the area they have the least amount of time (or budget) to devote to. To keep your team engaged, motivated and current, here are three ways to make development a part of each person's role.

First, if you've got the budget, send your people to conferences and industry events. Make sure the events are relevant to their roles and have them prepare a presentation for the rest of the team to share what they learned.

If springing for travel and conference fees isn't in the cards, consider getting a membership to online learning libraries such as Lynda.com. Have your team research courses of interest and plan a quarterly curriculum filled with these and a few you assign yourself to address any weak spots.

Finally, for the no-cost option, start a daily "Inspiration of the week" email or a weekly lunch presentation where your team rotates sharing cool design resources, websites, or TED talks they've found. It turns out that allowing your team the time to keep learning doesn't take much time at all.

_____

Kim Kiser

Step-by-Step: A Seat at the Table

Business people like to throw the word "creative" around, but in most marketing departments, the creative team—the in-house design group—is undervalued. Creative teams are often seen as nothing more than a post-decision, means-to-an-end resource to get the work done. We are overlooked when business decisions are first outlined and eventually finalized.

Graphic designers are, by nature, creative problem solvers
Creative problem solving is a skill that can be applied to all aspects of business, and at all times. But the big question is, how do we get a seat at the table? How do we get involved in the meetings and conversations? We're the workhorses, not invited and often not wanted, so how do we show that we're capable of more?

Like all good graphic designers, I went "big picture" first, but with purpose. I looked at the situation from the leadership's perspectives. Their hard work and dedication paid off because they had the opportunity to contribute, to set the tone and make the decisions. They wouldn't just let the creative team in because I asked, or because I personally felt I would be an asset. The meeting room was already full of opinions, and adding another voice (already seen as an outsider) could possibly make things worse. And, honestly, I was already known for having a strong personality and not backing down. Would I be a nuisance? Perhaps. But that didn't mean my impact couldn't be helpful. It turns out the best decisions come from disruption. By management giving me the opportunity to become part of the strategy discussions, it made our projects and team more successful.

The biggest challenge?
Timing. Our timeline was seen as a "slowdown" in the process, through no fault of our own. My creative group is, by default, at the end of the production timeline. We're the last stop before the door, so by the time the project comes across our desks, it is already late. Since our deadlines are typically based on customer ship dates, asking for more

time is never an option. We're already under scrutiny, and we've just started. The only way to change this timing problem is to have a broader vision of what the company is working on well before it's in my lap. I want to see the pipeline from inception and be involved from Day One to properly judge priorities.

Armed with this information, I approached the VP of Marketing and stated Creative needed to be part of the decision making from the beginning. In order to minimize his worry that I would just be another opinion in an already burdened process, I proactively offered to be "a fly on the wall." I was only there to listen, not to contribute. I just wanted to hear the conversations.

Instead of asking for a seat at the table, I asked for access to the conversation. I asked for the ability to listen, and listening can be as powerful as talking.

It worked. Very few VPs will turn down someone's request to attend MORE meetings. I viewed it as prioritizing my team's time with the best and most complete knowledge I could gather.

I was then invited to the marketing planning meeting. Just like I promised, I sat in the room and took notes. I took notes on what would affect my team, but also on how people responded to in-meeting feedback. It not only turned into a lesson on production timelines but also on personality and workflow.

After a few meetings I started having a broader understanding and felt more comfortable with the marketing team as a whole. While I still did not speak up in the meetings, I did do one thing differently—I began speaking with the people after the meetings. If I agreed with a viewpoint, I would throw my (then not-asked-for) support in the ring, privately. I would reinforce their opinions, and I would also engage in a deeper discussion. Remember: Creatives are "big picture," and my colleagues used my perspective almost immediately.

From the backend, my colleagues then changed my meeting involvement. These people started asking me what my opinion was during the meetings. In the beginning, I maintained a team-building stance. I would only build on something someone else said. I did not want to blow up an idea; I just wanted to support what was already being discussed. This way I was not seen as disagreeable, just supportive. Over time, I was able to actually throw out alternatives and disagree with other views.

The key?
Time and patience, as well as assuming some risk. Importantly, I had to deliver on my original promise and prove that being part of the full process was making my team more effective.

How did that happen?
Again, risk. We would need to work on projects before they were 100% approved. We would be working on projects that may not launch, meaning that our time could technically be wasted. However, we were always ahead of the project. Nothing ever landed in my lap without me knowing the full project and its timeline, and that was worth the risk and the "wasted" time. Having additional time and buy-in to do the project right completely changed the quality of the work. Now not only are we meeting our deadlines, but we are also delivering better work. And that "wasted" time? It allowed my team to get experience, stretch themselves and learn to handle failure better.

Finally, by far the most important part was follow-through. I needed to make sure that my boss knew the outcome and subsequent improvements. He had taken a risk in inviting me to be part of the high-level meetings, and I wanted to communicate that he'd made a great, department-changing decision. I systematically kept detailed notes on both my time and my team's time, and I presented how our ability to hit deadlines had dramatically improved and how our team was better informed and responsible for product success. I shared awards we had won and the many glowing reviews we'd received from co-workers, both in Marketing and elsewhere in the company.

But I won't sugarcoat it: This process is never-ending. I am constantly looking at ways to keep my team on the front lines. The more we can contribute to the company's success, the more opportunities we will be presented with. Big picture? It is not an easy path, but it is extremely rewarding.

Jim Woods
Creative Director
Spectrum Brands

Jim Woods is the Creative Director of Spectrum Brands Aquatic division, makers of pretty much everything related to fish, aquariums, ponds and reptiles. If you've ever bought a Tetra, Marineland, Instant Ocean, Jungle or any of another half dozen brands of fish stuff, you've bought the work of Jim and his team. He and his department create the collateral surrounding Spectrum's entire industry leading aquatic brands. They also contribute to research and development, influence product design and consult on business decisions outside the traditional role of graphic designers.

For the past six years Jim has had the pleasure of sharing his experiences as a speaker at national and local design conferences. Most recently he has been an instructor at Radford University for package design. Prior to working with Spectrum, Jim worked for the Baltimore and Washington, DC division of Clear Channel Communications and has over 17 years of in-house design experience.

2-MINUTE TIP

Staying Connected to Remote Teams

If you are working for a large organization, it's likely you've got creative teams spread out—within the city, across the country and/or around the globe. While the industry stays connected via technology, it can still prove challenging to keep remote teams informed, engaged and connected. A three-pronged approach can help bridge your teams together.

First, identify someone in each location, often the traffic manager, to send a weekly job list to the remote teams. This is particularly important for global teams so the regional teams know what projects are in the works that will likely head their way to adapt.

Second, have monthly creative calls in which everyone posts work, either to a SharePoint site or via WebEx, to review major projects for the month, highlighting successes and things that could have gone better. If you can hop on a video conference for these calls, all the better.

Lastly, nothing beats face-to-face interactions. As a leader, visiting remote teams on an annual basis goes a long way toward staying connected. If that isn't always practical, identify key employees throughout the year to spend a week with the larger team to collaborate on high-priority initiatives. The knowledge they bring back to their teams and the relationships they form help keep communication lines open.

Kim Kiser

DISCUSSION:
Alberta Testanero + Robin Colangelo

Alberta Testanero

Creative Leader

Fashion Industry In-House Guru

Five professional women who never met before took a blind trip to amazing Ireland and met for the first time at JFK Airport in New York City. And that's how I met Alberta.

Alberta always has a great smile, is easy to talk to and is loads of fun. So I asked her if she would be willing to talk to me about her in-house experience over the years in the fashion industry.

We met for a drink on a dreary Wednesday evening after work and giggled our butts off over several glasses of Rioja. Here's what I learned as we sunk into swapping in-house stories:

Are you noticing any new in-house trends?
The obvious trend is that digital teams are getting larger and the print teams are becoming smaller.

Where do you find leadership inspiration?
I've had some great managers, but the ones I wanted to please the most, who got the best work from me, were the ones who made me feel comfortable and not afraid of sharing what may be at first a silly idea. Leaders who get their hands dirty themselves, who you can learn from, are always going to inspire. They gain respect, therefore creating a team that wants to do the best work. If you don't respect your manager, you're not going to do your best work.

How do you set the tone for your team?
I like to keep it light. The key word is team. I want people to be happy with what they're doing and not be afraid to speak up if they're not. Personalities are as important as talent, and I make sure when putting a team together that everyone is a good fit. There's no room for design divas.

Do you use outside agencies in the fashion industry?

I actually have seen it specifically in fashion as of late. I've seen a move toward outside agencies for fashion ad campaigns. Perhaps there is a notion that agencies have more pull with the big photographers and production companies. I can't say for sure, because I myself haven't been in that position.

What's been your biggest in-house challenge?

The actual amount of work that an in-house team (at least at a global retail company) cranks out weekly is amazing. You really have to be great at multitasking.

What has surprised you the most about being in-house?

Actual job satisfaction. When I first went in-house I didn't know what to expect. Would it be as exciting? The answer is yes. And when you can focus on one brand, and really feel ownership, it can be extremely gratifying. **When you put your heart and soul into a brand you love, you're going to do good work.**

What's the largest career hurdle you ever had to overcome?

I wouldn't say this is a career hurdle, but once you're in-house at a global brand, you can become labeled for retail so it's difficult to move into an agency afterwards. I don't know many people who have made the switch.

Have the in-house teams you have been a part of functioned like in-house agencies?

Yes, definitely. Our clients are Marketing, Licensing, Design, Visual Merchandising, PR, etc. We have Account Managers who represent those clients (part of our in-house team) and then the jobs move through Creative just as they would at an agency. Everyone's roles and responsibilities are very specific, and with the high volume of work we churn out, it helps to keep everyone efficient. We have the same roles and functions as an agency: from Junior Designers to Creative Directors, Traffic Managers, Account Managers, Project Managers, Print Production, Art Buyers, plus photographers and retouchers.

Did you always know you wanted to be a part of the fashion industry?

Not at all. It was kind of a fluke. I worked at small branding studios developing logos and corporate identities when I first got out of college, but after a few years I was offered a job at Kate Spade when it was still a start-up. I didn't actually look for a job in fashion, but it suited me, and now I prefer this industry over others.

Looking back 10 years, what would you change about your career path?

If I could change one thing, I would have gotten into digital sooner. I love paper and printed ephemera and find working in print more creatively satisfying than working in digital. But sadly, there's just not as much print around anymore. It won't die completely, but there are fewer and fewer full-time print positions in our field.

Do you think the in-house industry is missing anything that we need in the future to be successful?

We need some good PR! I love being part of an in-house team. The work is great, and I've been on award-winning teams. But I think when people hear in-house they may think it's not as cool, or the people couldn't make it at an agency, but that can't be further from the truth.

Thanks, Alberta, I think you are our good PR!

A little more about Alberta

Alberta Testanero is a creative director and graphic designer whose passions are branding, art direction, typography and letterpress. Originally from New England, but a New Yorker for the past two decades, she has worked with inspiring and influential brands including Tiffany & Co., Coach, Reed Krakoff, Jo Malone London, Kate Spade, Jack Spade, Waterworks and more. Some of her most notable projects include designing the debut Kate Spade custom stationery line and the Kate Spade Etiquette three-book series, as well as creating the brand identities and packaging for Coach, Reed Krakoff and Jack Spade. Whether art directing a catalog or designing an invitation or award-winning logo, Alberta approaches every project with infectious enthusiasm and a keen eye for details.

Creating a
Career Strategy

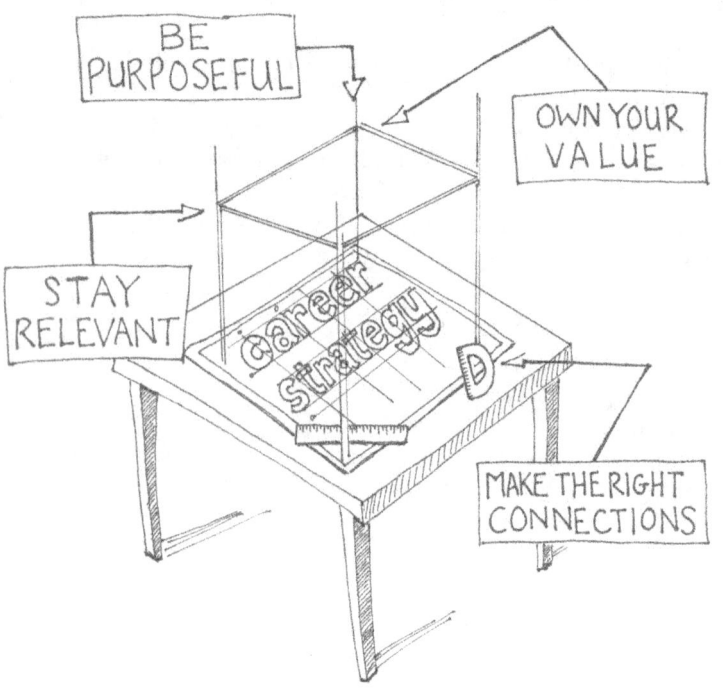

Too often people don't realize a successful career strategy requires a plan. To create a plan with a solid foundation, consider the following:

Be purposeful

You have to know where you want to go and get ready. Without a purpose, you won't be able to achieve anything. I know you hear people say all the time some unknowable entity made this happen or "I just got lucky." That sounds great until you remember one of the definitions of luck is "when preparation meets opportunity."

Own your value—not your ego

Successful career strategies include publicizing your achievements. Your value comes from your experience and your intellect. Remind people of your accomplishments, why you are here today and where you are going next. When you own your experiences and share your intellect, people will see you as someone who should move forward and, in turn, they will help you get there.

Develop your trust circle

You have got to know who your friends are! More than friends, these are your professional allies. They are the ones you trust with your career who can give you sound business advice when you are thinking about a career move, how to navigate a work situation or how to improve your work relationships. This is the group that is objective, successful and loyal.

Connect with the right people

Connect with the right person, or people, within the company. The "right people" are those individuals in the company who can help advance your career. You know them because they usually have the corner office. How you connect with them is by finding a common interest or lending your expertise to a project. This will get you in their sights, publicize your talents and give you an entrance into the inner circle of your company.

Elevate the conversation about yourself

It's important to talk about yourself in a positive light and about your accomplishments. Remember that you are a great business partner to the people you work for and with.

Stay relevant

Stay abreast of the trends, changes and growth in your area of expertise, and business in general. Continuing to learn by reading the trades and business news is one way of educating yourself. Conferences and industry events are another. It could also mean unlearning what you already know to make space for what's new and what's next.

Once you know what you want to do, and who can help you do it, then you have a foundation for figuring out your plan of action—your personal career bible. Your plan of action will include characteristics of the career you're striving for, a timeline, who you will partner with to achieve the goal, financial goals and an exit.

Create your career map

Create steps of achievement, AKA your career map. To draw your map, gather information from your trusted circle, research others who've achieved the titles of success, read the trades, attend events and get input that supports your goals. Once you've finished drawing your career map, it will be the place you go back to when you are feeling lost.

In summary, stay focused—make sure at least four to six hours out of your day are activities in pursuit of your goal. The decisions you make should revolve around one simple question: "Is what I am doing helping me attain my desired goal?" Finally, to keep your career on track, create a timeline to achieve your success. Consider how long it will take you to achieve your goals, accounting for a few bumps in the road, and ask yourself how long you are willing to work toward this goal.

Nathalie Heywood Smith
Career Strategist + Recruitment

Nathalie Heywood Smith has created and executed thought leadership, reputation management and social media programs. She has helped professionals transition into new careers, graduates embark on their career journey and executives position themselves for emerging growth. Former Vice President at Update Inc., she started the division Update Creative and directed all business development and strategy for the recruiting firm.

Lessons Learned

LESSON 1: Have a back-up plan
It was the week after New Year's 2009 with the economy at
a low. I was VP, Creative Director at Christie's auction house and
expecting the arrival of my first daughter. After 12 years, I went
in one day and found myself out of a job due to a
company-wide restructure.

LESSON 2: Prioritize your schedule
Not everything can be first on your to-do list. Achieving professional
and parental success is a constant exercise of focus, determination
and humor. For me, becoming a parent honed my perspective. I am
fortunate to have great partners at work and at home, enabling me
to be present for my family and deliver results at the office.

LESSON 3: Never doubt yourself
While I was out of a job I never considered myself unemployed.
Instead, I always considered myself a Creative Director. I was
fortunate to have access to a job placement/coaching agency.
I didn't hesitate to apply when I saw a posting for Director, Creative
Services at Lincoln Center for the Performing Arts (LCPA). The
description sounded perfect, and I submitted my resume. On the
suggestion of my coach, I contacted a colleague from my former
company who had ties to LCPA and a phone interview was
scheduled. I researched everything about the organization and
took a tour to be prepared for the interviews. Less than four months
later I was working at the world's leading performing arts center.

LESSON 4: Go the distance
Beginning a job at a new company is starting over in many ways.
You were hired because of your experience, your portfolio, your
personality and what value and ideas you can bring to the company.
You then need to deliver. It doesn't happen overnight. It takes time
to establish trust and build solid working relationships with your
team and internal clients, up to the president. You can't rest on

your last success. Your influence and mark into the visual representation of the organization needs time to develop and unfold in all areas. Attend to details. It won't go unnoticed. I once delivered a presentation box to a prospective donor's residence, following the doorman to the freight elevator to make sure that the box content stayed intact.

LESSON 5: Evolve your style
Working at LCPA pushed my creation process. I came from an environment where the art object was served by a clean design aesthetic, a style I personally favor. At LCPA, the design must convey the exuberance of live performance. Success required learning to collaborate with artistic directors to transfer their visions into seasonal campaigns. It took time to develop an identity for each of LCPA's many performance series in a way that together express the LCPA brand, whether it is an elegant solution for traditional classical music or vibrant representation of a large outdoors dance festival. Exploring new visual vocabularies beyond my natural comfort zone allowed me to evolve professionally.

LESSON 6: Give space to create
You can have all the ideas in the world, but you need a good team to help you bring them to life. Not only skill, innovation and experience but also a good personality is key. The chemistry needs to be right. Just like in an orchestra, everyone fulfills a special role. I once attended a lecture of the CEO of the American Red Cross who stressed the importance of only having the very best staff. It put things for me into perspective. You can manage staff to a certain point, but the readiness has to come from the team member. You want individuals who possess a heightened sense of responsibility to get the job done. I like to keep an environment where staff can focus on creating and producing with little distraction. It's rewarding to see your staff succeed bringing great concepts and design together.

LESSON 7: Partner with the best

One wonders sometimes, how it would be working on the agency side, having a number of different clients. At LCPA, projects aside from new initiatives, usually revolve on a seasonal basis, yet no year has been the same since I started. I have experienced working with agencies, which has been a positive process as well as eye-opening. There can be a good project distribution between in-house and an agency. The agency should be hired to do the work they do best. For example, at LCPA we establish the seasonal identities for our programs in-house and the agency executes the advertisements. It is a streamlined process, which allows the time to attend to new initiatives. There is also a fresh angle that an agency can provide. When LCPA underwent a rebranding I learned a lot in the process working with an agency. At times it takes an outside perspective to see beyond what is in front of you. Further, I have collaborated with illustrators on a per project basis, which has been a great experience and always enhances the product. As designers, unless illustration is your forte, our illustration skills are at times limited. I admire illustrators who excel in their custom style and medium.

LESSON 8: Find your niche

I have been fortunate to work in the arts in both the profit and not-for-profit sectors. At Christie's, I was exposed to some of the greatest works of art up close and witnessed auction world records set in the sale rooms, basically experiencing an art history education as part of my role of leading the in-house design team. Now, at LCPA I see some of the world's greatest artists on stage, learning from my passionate colleagues about different music and performance genres. There is something special and unique about working in-house. You become part of an organization that is made of different departments, working together to accomplish the organization's mission. Projects can accelerate and be completed at a fast pace.

Martin Schott
Creative Director
Lincoln Center for the Performing Arts

Martin Schott is Creative Director, at Lincoln Center for the Performing Arts, one of 11 resident organizations on Lincoln Center's 16.3 acre campus. He is responsible for developing creative visual strategies to support Lincoln Center's brand identity, including programming (American Songbook, Great Performers, Lincoln Center Festival, Lincoln Center Out of Doors, Midsummer Night Swing, Mostly Mozart Festival, White Light Festival and "Live from Lincoln Center"), fundraising and education.

Prior to his current role, Martin worked at Christie's auction house, where he served as Vice President and Creative Director of the Americas, developing marketing initiatives for some of the most expensive fine art, jewelry, furniture and decorative arts ever sold at auction. Martin grew up in Switzerland and graduated from Art Center College of Design in Pasadena.

Delegating

Running a creative team takes spinning a lot of plates—from directing the work to overseeing budgets to balancing workloads, not to mention answering emails and attending meetings. It's easy for these day-to-day tasks to bubble to the top of your to-do list, leaving tasks such as staff development and team building, which are no less important, to languish at the bottom.

This is where delegating can step in. If you have a weak performer on your team, assign them a buddy—someone doing a great job in a similar role—to coach them. Having trouble keeping your team informed and connected? Identify key employees to plan and run monthly show-and-tell meetings.

Delegating gives your top performers growth opportunities, promotes a more collaborative work environment and eases some stress on your busy schedule.

You can't do everything. The important thing is to remember that you don't have to.

_____

Kim Kiser

A Fork in the Road of Your Career Path: How To Avoid Being "Petered"

"The Peter Principle" is defined as follows: In every hierarchical job (corporate or otherwise) you will eventually be promoted to a level of incompetence—meaning after you've sat in the chair longer than anyone else, you will be asked to raise to the next level whether or not you're ready, experienced, qualified—or you even want it—and you will eventually fail. That is, unless you read this article and discover how to avoid it.

New and even established in-house teams don't always have a set career path. Oftentimes they were born out of necessity, and no one thought past that. "Let's hire some people and, well, we'll figure it out as we go." And as business grows and/or as you start taking on more projects, the need arises to create a hierarchy within. There are some teams that have an already established hierarchy—this can happen there, too. I will quickly discuss four case studies of people I have seen rise up in the ranks of an in-house team and how/if/when The Peter Principle took hold.

CASE ONE: Master Production Artist rises to Production Manager and flops. Anarchy ensues.

Long story short—an amazing Production Artist, let's call him Steven impresses everyone with his skills. He's a perfectionist. Blood, sweat and tears. He makes friends with everyone. Super great hire. The world is happy. The Production Team gets too large and the Creative Director can no longer manage them all, so they need a Production Manager. Steven is excited about the promotion. Steven, however, has never managed anyone so he takes his perfectionist ways to a dictator level. Nothing is good enough for him. He takes over everyone's jobs. He's a horrible manager. People quit. He's eventually fired. He had a fork in his career and was flattered by it—not thinking of the next steps and what the job was really about. He wasn't ready for it. Steven got Petered!

CASE TWO: Amazing Designer turns Creative Director and is really good at it, but hates it and misses being a Designer. Anarchy ensues.

An amazing Designer, let's call her Ethel. Everyone loved her. Ethel had "manager" written all over her. She was a natural leader. People looked up to her. There was a fork in her career path when she was asked to become Creative Director and oversee a lot of designers. She was brilliant at it, but she hated it. It sucked everything creative out of her. She felt like a sell-out. All she wanted to do was design. She quit. She became a designer elsewhere. Ethel got Petered, though hers was less about incompetence and more about not meeting her desires. She didn't think through the promotion.

CASE THREE: Amazing Art Director is asked to move to Creative Director. Says "No." Anarchy is happily avoided.

An amazing Art Director, let's call her Amy, loved working closely with designers and photographers. Amy was very well spoken and loved her job. She got to direct, design, illustrate and manage only two people. Everyone was so happy with her performance that when the Creative Director position opened up, they were excited to give it to her. More money, eight people to manage and more involvement with executives. She turned it down—twice. The thought of not being able to design and being bogged down by corporate executives and managing eight people turned her off. She was smart; she knew what she wanted and didn't let a fancy title or additional salary get in the way. She avoided getting Petered.

CASE FOUR: Graphic Designer turns Art Director turns Creative Director. So far, so good. The Peter Principle hasn't got him yet. Anarchy is on hold.

Another employee, let's call him Tommy, started as a Production Artist. He went from agency to in-house—getting promoted along the way to Designer, Senior Designer, Art Director and finally Creative Director.

Every step of the way he jumped right into new responsibilities, making sure that he clearly thought through all that was going to be asked of him. The biggest leap was early on when he was asked to manage a team of 12 and still design full time. Managing was new to him, but he didn't want to get Petered so he made sure to ask a lot of questions, read articles, watched TED talks and find a great mentor to help manage his transition. He knew he was moving to a role that he knew nothing about, so he absorbed as much as possible. In the end, after 11 years of managing large teams, he has avoided getting Petered because he made sure to learn.

Never stop learning. Establish a management style and be nimble and flexible. And most importantly–**MAKE SURE THAT YOU WANT IT.**

You may one day come to a fork in your career path and have to make the decision. Don't let fame, fortune and a fancy title get you Petered. Make sure you are ready for it. Remember why you fell in love with your career in the first place, and make sure the next step is one that will elevate you to where you want to go—one that will make you a better person, a happier person, a more satisfied person. It's OK to say no. Trust your gut. Trust yourself and don't trust any guy named Peter.

Jereme Clymer
Creative Director
P.F. Chang's

Jereme Clymer has (so far) survived a 17-year creative career. He has done his time at ad agencies and experienced the insomnia of being a full-time freelancer before falling in love with being a corporate sell-out, in-house creative. His true creative passion lies with creativity itself. He is constantly on the hunt for his sneaky and elusive inner child as well as the child inside everyone around him. He is currently the Creative Director for P.F. Chang's in Scottsdale, Arizona. He spends his free time with his wife and two kids, living a very happy, very stereotypical suburban life.

Special Acknowledgements

2-Minute Tips by Kim Kiser
Editorial Director, InSource
Vice President, Creative Director,
Dimensional Fund Advisors

After 17 years in New York, Kim Kiser relocated to Austin, Texas, in 2012 to join Dimensional Fund Advisors as Vice President, Creative Director, where she oversees the in-house editorial, design, video, digital and presentations teams. For most of the past decade, Kim served as Vice President, Global Creative Director for Morgan Stanley, where she managed the brand and oversaw print, Web and animation design produced in the firm's New York, London and Tokyo studios. Prior to Morgan Stanley, Kim worked on the agency side as an art director for the arts, biotech, finance and publishing industries.

With a bachelor's degree in Journalism from the University of Texas at Austin, Kim started her career as a copywriter, writing television, radio and print ads. She earned a master's degree in Communications Design from Pratt Institute, where she later taught Psychology of Visual Perception in the Graduate Communications Design department for eight years. In 2014, Kim was selected as one of the "People to Watch" by GDUSA. She has served as Editorial Director for InSource since 2009.

Illustrations by Mark Cole
Illustrator/Designer
mark your designs

An award-winning freelance illustrator established in digital and traditional fine art, Mark Cole, the Principal at mark your designs, produces custom illustrations and paintings, which have been recognized and distributed worldwide.

Mark has been commissioned to create designs for product, editorial and private illustrations and is well versed in just about any medium, from charcoal to watercolor to Photoshop and Illustrator. His talents allow him to illustrate from supplied photographs or still life, and his conceptual design process is as collaborative as his clients would like it to be.

Ever since Mark can remember, he spent most of his free time sketching and painting and gradually began taking on freelance illustration work, which evolved to building his own studio, named mark your designs.

With a strong visual and typographic sensibility, Mark is skilled in graphic design and custom signage design. He has honed his business and design management skills working for a high-end custom sign studio for the past decade.

Mark attended the University of Louisville for his bachelor's degree in Art and then went on to the School of Communication Arts to further his education in digital and graphic design.

Mark has received accolades from several prestigious design awards programs such as Hermes, HOW and GDUSA.

www.behance.net/markyourdesigns

A Little Back Story

InSource history

Since 2002, InSource has been committed to leadership excellence and effective business management in the ever-growing in-house creative community. Our membership has grown to reach thousands of in-house creatives around the globe, providing a platform to share best practices to enhance the value that in-house teams add to their organizations and brands.

Join us in our efforts to empower our teams and our peers in pursuit of design management excellence. Whether you're a leader or an aspiring leader, InSource is the professional resource for in-house creative teams.

Visit our website at in-source.org for more information on how you can make InSource a valuable resource for you and your team.

Together, we can inspire, foster communication and propel the in-house community forward!

Stay tuned for Leadership Volume Three coming in 2017.

If you would like to get involved in Volume Three,
contact Robin.colangelo@in-source.org.